How Coyote Stole Fire

by Bo Grayson
illustrated by Emilie Boon

 HOUGHTON MIFFLIN HARCOURT
School Publishers

Copyright © by Houghton Mifflin Harcourt Publishing Company

All rights reserved. No part of this work may be reproduced or transmitted in any form or by any means, electronic or mechanical, including photocopying or recording, or by any information storage and retrieval system, without the prior written permission of the copyright owner unless such copying is expressly permitted by federal copyright law. Requests for permission to make copies of any part of the work should be addressed to Houghton Mifflin Harcourt School Publishers, Attn: Permissions, 6277 Sea Harbor Drive, Orlando, Florida 32887-6777.

Printed in India

ISBN-13: 978-0-547-02297-0
ISBN-10: 0-547-02297-2

2 3 4 5 6 7 8 0940 18 17 16 15 14 13 12 11 10

If you have received these materials as examination copies free of charge, Houghton Mifflin Harcourt School Publishers retains title to the materials and they may not be resold. Resale of examination copies is strictly prohibited.

Possession of this publication in print format does not entitle users to convert this publication, or any portion of it, into electronic format.

Long ago people had no fire. In the winter, the wind was cold and snow fell. The people could not get warm.

Coyote saw that the people were cold and he wanted to help them.

Coyote knew that the Fire Beings lived at the top of a mountain. They kept fire there.

The top of the mountain was at a great height. But Coyote knew that fire could keep the people warm. So he went slowly toward the top of the mountain. When he reached the top, he crept close to the fire. Then he dug a tunnel and hid.

Coyote watched the Fire Beings take care of the fire. After some time, the fire burned out, and only warm embers were left. Then one Fire Being gathered small sticks. The other Fire Beings used these sticks to start the fire. Soon they made the fire roaring hot.

Coyote wanted to steal some fire for the people. But the Fire Beings guarded the fire day and night.

Coyote watched and watched. Then he saw that the Fire Beings were sleepy in the morning. They did not guard the fire very well right before the sun came up. So dawn was the best time to steal the fire.

But Coyote knew that he needed help. He went down from the mountain and spoke to his friends. Squirrel, Chipmunk, and Frog agreed to help. They made a clever plan to steal some fire.

The friends returned to the mountain. Frog waited at the bottom. Chipmunk waited halfway up the mountain. Squirrel waited just below the peak. Coyote crept alone toward the fire and hid in his tunnel. He waited for dawn.

Right before the sun came up, Coyote dashed out of his tunnel. He ran up and stole a piece of fire.

The Fire Beings woke up. "Stop that thief!" they cried. They pointed in his direction. "Grab that thief!"

One Fire Being grabbed his tail. When she touched it, the end turned white.

Coyote threw the fire to Squirrel. Squirrel caught the fire, but it was so hot that his tail curled up.

Squirrel threw the fire down the mountain to Chipmunk. Down raced the Fire Beings after the fire. One grabbed Chipmunk's back and left three marks.

Chipmunk threw the fire down the mountain to Frog. Down raced the Fire Beings after the fire. One grabbed Frog's tail. Frog leaped and left his tail behind.

Frog escaped with the fire. The Fire Beings roared in anger. Chipmunk, Squirrel, and Coyote ran down off the mountain. Then the four animal friends brought fire back to the people.

Coyote did not brag about stealing the fire. He showed the people how to use it. Now the people could keep warm in the winter.

The people noticed that Fire Beings had hurt the four friends. Coyote's tail had a white tip. Squirrel had a curly tail. Chipmunk's back had three stripes. And Frog had lost his tail.

The people did not tease the animals because they had changed. They thanked them for stealing fire. Then they helped them heal.

Responding

✓ TARGET SKILL **Understanding Characters** Is Coyote a kind character or an unkind character? Copy and complete the chart below.

Words	Actions	What I Know
He wanted to help them.	He ?	Coyote is ?

Write About It

Text to World Coyote and his friends help the people. Use a few sentences to write a summary essay about how Coyote helped the people. Then write about a time when you helped someone, and why it is important to help others. Include only the most important ideas from the story.

✓ TARGET VOCABULARY

brag	height
curled	tease
direction	toward
healed	tunnel

✓ **TARGET SKILL** **Understanding Characters** Tell more about characters.

✓ **TARGET STRATEGY** **Summarize** Stop to tell important events as you read.

GENRE A **folktale** is a story that is often told by people of a country.